I CAN BE A WRITER

I Can Be an Editor

Meeg Pincus

Published in the United States of America by:

CHERRY LAKE PRESS
2395 South Huron Parkway, Suite 200, Ann Arbor, Michigan 48104
www.cherrylakepress.com

Reading Adviser: Beth Walker Gambro, MS, Ed., Reading Consultant, Yorkville, IL

Photo Credits: © Dallasetta/Shutterstock, 5; © Ekaterina_Minaeva/Shutterstock, 6; © Kaspars Grinvalds/Shutterstock, 7; © Andrey_Popov/Shutterstock, 8; © Sebastian Crocker/Shutterstock, 9; © Ground Picture/Shutterstock, 11; © Brian A Jackson/Shutterstock, 12; © Prathankarnpap/Shutterstock, 13; © Calvin L. Leake/Dreamstime.com, 15; © Adylee/Dreamstime.com, 15 overlay; © Helder Almeida/Dreamstime.com, 16; © Luisa P Oswalt/Shutterstock, 18; © Cherry Lake Publishing Group, 20; © Pressmaster/Shutterstock, 21; © Mykola Sosiukin/Dreamstime.com, 22

Copyright © 2026 by Cherry Lake Publishing Group

All rights reserved. No part of this book may be reproduced or utilized in any form or by any means without written permission from the publisher.

Cherry Lake Press is an imprint of Cherry Lake Publishing Group.

Library of Congress Cataloging-in-Publication Data has been filed and is available at catalog.loc.gov

Cherry Lake Publishing Group would like to acknowledge the work of the Partnership for 21st Century Learning, a Network of Battelle for Kids. Please visit Battelle for Kids online for more information.

Printed in the United States of America

Note from publisher: Websites change regularly, and their future contents are outside of our control. Supervise children when conducting any recommended online searches for extended learning opportunities.

CONTENTS

What Do Editors Do?	4
Why Would I Want to Edit Writing?	10
How Can I Learn to Edit Writing?	17
Activity	22
Find Out More	23
About the Author	23
Glossary	24
Index	24

WHAT DO EDITORS DO?

Have you read any great books, magazines, comics, or websites? If so, was the language clear and all the spelling correct?

Then you've seen what editors do!

Editors help bring written **publications** to life. They're also "fixers" who make sure writing flows smoothly and is free from errors.

Editors help make sure a piece of writing is the best it can be.

Editors work on any kind of writing that's published, either on paper or online. There are different kinds of editors in the writing world.

In the Spiderman universe, J. Jonah Jameson is the editor of the *Daily Bugle*. Jameson decides what kind of stories the paper will tell about Spiderman.

　First, there are editors who manage publications. These editors choose the best stories to tell, such as which books to publish or which news stories to share in a newspaper. Then they help bring the stories to print.

Another group of editors fix writing before it is published. They dig into the details of a written piece to make sure it reads as well as possible.

Think!

Can you think of another kind of editor you know about? What makes them similar or different from editors of writing?

These editors check if paragraphs and sentences flow smoothly. They may move parts around in a story or help a writer improve a **plot** or character. They correct any spelling, **punctuation**, or **grammar** mistakes.

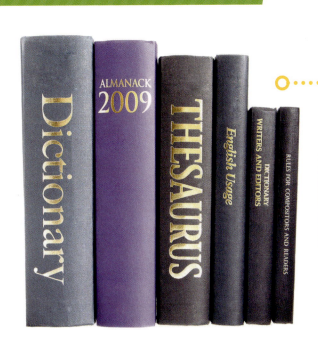

Good editors rely on reference texts and style guides to help strengthen writing.

9

WHY WOULD I WANT TO EDIT WRITING?

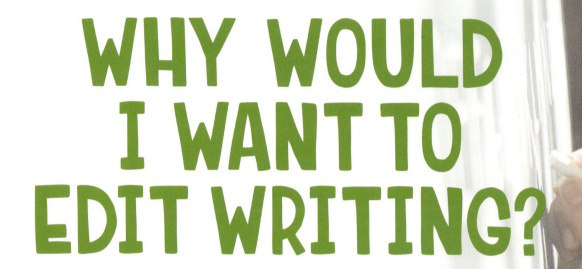

Would you like to work with writers and others to bring stories to life? Do you enjoy figuring out the puzzles and learning the rules of language? Are you a strong speller and reader? Then you may want to be an editor!

Ask Questions!

Write a letter to an editor of a book or other publication you like. Ask them why they decided to become an editor. Ask what they like most about editing writing. Ask anything you like!

Teachers must be clear and encouraging, too.

Editors are helpers to writers. They must be able to tell writers what they've done well and what they can improve. They should be clear and encouraging as they do this.

Many people think editors work alone. But they actually work with many people through the editing process. They may work with **literary agents**, **art directors**, illustrators, or salespeople. People who love writing and work well with others make great editors!

Editors are also problem solvers. As an editor, you use creative and **critical thinking**. Like a detective, your job is to figure out what's going on with a piece of writing and spot anything out of place. This also means knowing language rules.

Editors make writing stronger. They check for spelling and grammar errors. They help polish the writing, or perfect it. So if you enjoy improving things, as well as learning and focusing on language details, you might like to be an editor.

Look!

Keep your eye out in daily life for errors on signs or in publications. You'll find them everywhere! Make it into a game with friends or family to sharpen your editing eye.

Can you spot the mistake on this sign?

15

HOW CAN I LEARN TO EDIT WRITING?

Editors are also readers. To help others with their writing, editors must read often and understand what makes writing appeal to readers.

Read a lot of the kind of writing you might like to edit. Maybe it's fiction stories, or newspapers, or even comic books—just read many of them! The more you read, the more you naturally understand good writing.

How many words can you find on the board? Use only letters that connect to each other in order.

18

To be an editor, you also must understand the **mechanics** of writing. This means learning the rules of grammar, spelling, and punctuation.

Word games are also a great tool for editor skill-building. Playing them can help you sharpen your mind and think about language more deeply. Seek-and-find games are good practice for spotting errors, too!

Make a Guess!

Why do you think we have rules of grammar, spelling, and punctuation?

Editors use proofreading marks like these when they edit text.

ℓ	delete
◯	fix spelling
≡	capitalize
/	lowercase
∧	insert
⊙	add period
#	add space
◡	close space

You can take classes in all kinds of writing. You can read your classmates' and friends' writing. See if you can find ways to make it even better. You can practice sharing your thoughts in ways that encourage others.

Can you be an editor? If you want to learn to help writers bring their stories to life with the best writing possible…yes, you can!

ACTIVITY

Practice being an editor with these sentences!

- Can you find the spelling errors in this sentence?

    Maria desided to stay home and read a book insted of playing owtside.

- Can you find the grammar errors in this sentence?

    His friends is going to the movies afternoon tomorrow.

- Can you find the punctuation errors in this sentence?

    When the girls cat got stuck in the tree she yelled Help.

- Can you make this sentence sound more exciting for a story?

    They heard a sound at night.

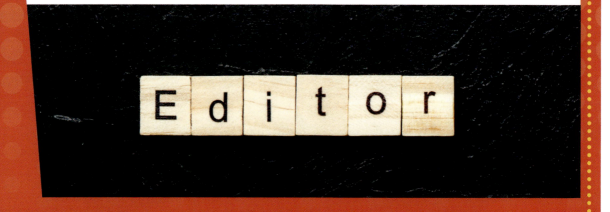

FIND OUT MORE

Books

Fiedler, Heidi. *The Know-Nonsense Guide to Grammar.* Beverly, MA: Walter Foster Publishing, 2022.

Kephart, Beth. *Good Books for Bad Children: The Genius of Ursula Nordstrom.* New York, NY: Anne Schwartz Books, 2023.

Websites

With an adult, explore more online with these suggested searches.

"15+ Best Grammar Games for Kids That are Super Fun!" *SplashLearn*

How to Be a Children's Book Editor, *DC Public Library*

ABOUT THE AUTHOR

Meeg Pincus loves to write. She is the author of more than 30 books for children. She has been a writer and editor for books, newspapers, magazines, and more. She also loves to sing, make art, and hang out with her family, friends, and adorable dog.

GLOSSARY

art directors (AHRT duh-REK-ters) creative professionals who manage the visual style of a publication

critical thinking (KRIH-tih-kuhl THINK-ing) process of questioning and interpreting information

grammar (GRAH-mer) language rules that govern how words are used and arranged

literary agents (LIH-tuh-rair-ee AY-juhnts) people who represent writers and their work to publishers and editors

mechanics (mih-KAH-niks) machinery or working parts of something

plot (PLAHT) series of events that make up a story

publications (puh-bluh-KAY-shuhns) written works that are made available to the public

punctuation (puhnk-chuh-WAY-shuhn) system of symbols used to separate words, phrases, and sentences for clear meaning

INDEX

activities, 22

communication skills, 4, 9, 10, 12–14, 21
content choices, 6, 7
copyediting, 8–9, 20
critical thinking, 14

editors, 4–9, 10–14, 17–21, 22
education, 21

errors, 4, 9, 14, 15, 19, 22

feedback, 12, 21

grammar and punctuation, 9, 14, 19, 22

learning, 17–21

newspaper editors, 6, 7

problem solving, 14
proofreading marks, 20
publication editors, 6, 7
punctuation and grammar, 9, 14, 19, 22

reading habits, 16–17
reference texts, 9

spelling, 4, 9, 10, 14, 15, 18, 19, 22

teamwork, 7–8, 12–13

word games, 18, 19

24